Meet Jim!

Written by
Barbara Catchpole

Meet Jim. Jim is a fish.
Look at him! He is all goo!

Can Jim jog?

Ha! Ha! Look at him!
Can you see legs?
Can you see feet?

No! Jim has no legs or feet.
Jim is all goo!

Jim cannot jog or hop
or run.
Jim cannot go up or down.

Jim is not a jack-in-a-box.
He is not quick.

For sure, Jim has no jacket and no top.

And look! He has no shorts and no boots!

No fuss, Jim!

Is Jim a fighter?

Can Jim fight?

No, Jim cannot fight. He is all goo. He cannot jab and he cannot hit!

Jim is looking for food.
But Jim has no teeth.

Can he get a jar of jam?
Can he cook food?

No. Jim has no teeth at all.

Jim sucks fish in – but not big fish.

I can check but I am sure
that Jim has no teeth!

You and I might meet Jim near the boats.

Jim will be wet.
And he will be all goo.

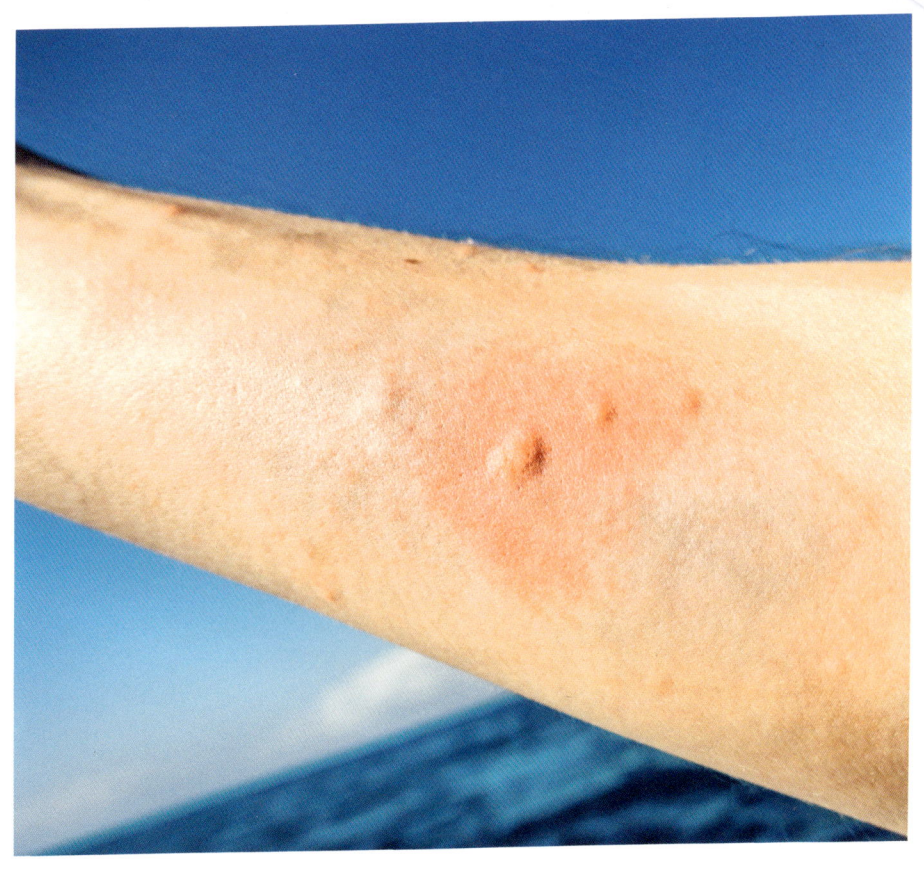

I might not see Jim,
but I might feel him.

Yes, I might feel Jim.
I might feel a bit of pain.

Jim might hurt me!